Wine on a Dime a Non Grape Alternative to Fantastic Wine

INTRODUCTION

When it Comes to Wines, for years, dating back to the beginning of time, Wine has always been around. Both White and Grape Wines can be made in different varieties from grapes that Originate from all over the world.

For anyone that has Purchased wines the Pricing can go from just a few Dollars to Several of thousands of dollars per bottle depending on the vintage of the Wine. Not everyone develops a Wine Palate and that's OK, however this can be extremely awkward at a higher end Restaurant, and Personally I've never let this get to me because I cannot stand the taste of a Strong Red Wines, tasting Similar to Vinegar I can think of many other beverages in it's Place. With this said, I bring to you my book, **Wine on a dime a Non Grape alternative to fantastic Wines** *as an alternative for a tasty adult beverage with a very Similar body but in flavors more Pleasant to the mouth if Grapes are not your thing.*

Fruit Wine, Called Country Wines is often thought of as redneck wine or the "Poor persons Wine" please do not let the name of Country wine throw you off, there's nothing wrong with making or enjoying it. I hope you enjoy this outline of making Wine yourself, I know I have it's been a very Rewarding Journey.

CHAPTERS

CHAPTER I

When it Comes to Crafting your own Wines It's important to understand the laws involved before doing so and I'd Like to discuss a couple of things before getting into the Science of Wine-making so that you may enjoy this Craft without making any errors that could create a headache. My best advice before getting started is to do an online search in your area of whats allowed/not allowed when it comes to making homemade wines at home.

In many Locations in the United States the Law allows each adult in the household to make up to 100 Gallons of home-brew per year providing it's for your own consumption and under no circumstances you try to sell it, that's the fine line of where it becomes Illegal (Selling without proper permits and Licenses).check with your Local to see for sure on the amount allowed to be made in the household. Because Wine is an alcoholic Beverage it's also a Responsibility to not serve to anyone under 21 years of age, doing so can have legal ramifications.

Beer has very Similar laws and Regulations as Wine and Similar Quantities can be made from home per adult per year. As a side note if you do decide to get into this exciting craft, I would not recommend Talking about the Craft to strangers because if and when they find out you can make either beverage it wouldn't surprise me if you were asked, Could you make me Some.. Don t do it, you never know the strangers intentions!

Legalities Continued -

Wine-making is a Craft that in time as the satisfaction builds its not uncommon to want to move on to greater or better things so I wanted to also touch on something I have heard while shopping for yeast in craft brewing stores.

Distilling of Spirits Is Illegal unless you have proper Licenses and permits. With local reality shows on discovery it may raise the eye of Curiosity thinking about Copper Stills and Spirits but it is illegal to distill spirits even if for home use only stay with beer and wine, and should you become bored with wine-making why not come up with your own recipes and experiment it's a great way to keep it fun. Now that we have talked do and don't so lets dig into wine-making!

CHAPTER II

The Start of any Great wine is sanitized equipment. Failure to Sanitize equipment religiously Can Produce Bacteria and off Tastes to be transferred to wine as you proceed with your Recipe. For this I cannot stress enough how important food grade Buckets are.

I highly recommend Two 5 gallon Buckets to be Used for Sanitizing only and when not in use keep the lids secured on them. Never use bleach inside the buckets as bleach permeated plastic and will transfer to your wine-making equipment, instead I recommend Solutions Such as the Sanitizing Solution Below to always be kept on hand to clean equipment with.

Cleaning Continued -

Star San, is a personal favorite sanitizer that I have used for years and It Can be had in almost any wine-making Supply Stores, you can never have two much of this, I keep a small crate of it on-hand for my wine-making Purposes.

In the interest of Cleanliness I highly recommend locating some safe areas in your home for both fermentation and Storage of your Equipment. When fermenting wine its very easy to accidentally transfer smells to the wine causing off flavors once finished so areas to avoid are (Kitchen) as you don't want your first batch of fruit wine to taste Like fried bacon, or to have it Taste like Fabric Softener (Laundry rooms). Its a best practice that any time you take an SG. (Specific Gravity) reading mix a new batch of must up or rack your wine to get in the hobbit of mixing one half a bucket of sanitizer up to immediately sterilize tools before putting them away

As crazy as this sounds, before getting into the craft think of it as bringing that new puppy home, having a plan in place of where to keep things. If your Home is fortunate enough to have a basement a great place is under the staircase in the basement or if you own a two story home under the staircase going upstairs is great, darkness being the key to let that wine ferment! Once you have Located an area be sure to find a small sheet of plywood or a large tray/pan to put under your ferment-er, its never a good idea to leave the carboy on a hard concrete floor or tile you need to insulate with a piece of material to avoid temp swings

CHAPTER III

Equipment in Wine-Making,

As you progress in the hobby it never hurts to get larger fermenter's, larger Carboys and More bottles and Corks, but careful Planning is essential to preserving your work so you don't have to immediately drink it or pour out. In this Chapter I want to go over the equations of your production as well as looking at the minimum equipment needed for your wine-making.

The Equations-
For Every one gallon batch of Wine made, this will fill five (750 ml) glass one bottles so below is a simplified reference on bottles needed

(1) Gallon of Wine is (5) 750 ml Glass Bottles of Wine

(2) Gallons of Wine is (10) 750 ml Glass Bottles of Wine

(3) Gallons of Wine is (15) 750 ml Glass Bottles of Wine

(4) Gallons of Wine is (20) 750 ml Glass Bottles of wine

(5) Gallons of Wine is (25) 750 ml Glass Bottles of Wine

With this equation you can easily select the quantity you desire and start Gathering materials for your first batch of Wine. I highly Recommend your first batch be (1) Gallon so if this is not for you, then you have not wasted money.

Please note that the materials list is complete but I have put a Star in front of bare minimum necessities to get Started. You will need a corker either way which can always be resold later if wine-making is not for you

MATERIALS LIST-

***1) Fermenting Bucket-** *I Started with a two gallon Plastic food-grade bucket with the lid. Please note, the Lid has a rubber bung already installed and this bung accepts the airlock to allow the bucket to release gas as the Must (Solution of Juice and sugar) is added and yeast is pitched we will discuss in a later chapter the process. The bucket also features a spigot to allow for easy bottle filling at a later time.*

*2) AIR LOCK-

The Purpose of the Air lock is to safely release the CO2 buildup in the Fermenter and to keep debris and insects out of your wine. When making Fruit Wines it's not uncommon to see fruit-flies attempting to find a way in, the airlock prevents this. To use the airlock pop the cap off the top and fill with water, you will have to twist it slightly to move water to both sides,

fill to the lines on each side. When you read on the internet everyone will say to add something different to the airlock, IE: Simple Syrup, Vodka, etc.. the problem with Vodka is that if the alcohol drops into the wine too early it will begin to kill off the yeast prematurely. By using simple syrup if it drips into the must, the yeast will go crazy possibly boiling out the top of the airlock, stay with Water!

Air Lock shown with rubber bung

the Rubber bung is designed to Fit into the insides of most Glass jugs. I personally use one gallon Jugs for my carboys

*3) GLASS CARBOYS-

a Carboy is used primarily for Second fermentation's along with racking your wine (Term meaning Moving from one Carboy to the next in an effort to get the wine off of your yeast sediment.)..after the first fermentation which is typically 25-45 days its time to rack your wine or (transfer it)to a clean carboy. **The way you can tell the first fermentation has completed is the intense bubbling in the airlock will slow to one bubble every 30 seconds or so..** *once you Rack your wine you should be cleaning the sediment out of original carboy and transferring it..*

**Glass Carboy Pictured,
steam from hot water/Sanitizing**

4) SIPHON PUMP-

A siphon pump is used in transferring or racking wine from fermenter to carboy, then carboy to carboy. Its very useful in getting clear wine, and I recommend on the end of the vinyl tubing that goes into the wine to tie a bamboo skewer one inch below the edge of tubing to make sure you don't transfer yeast sediments

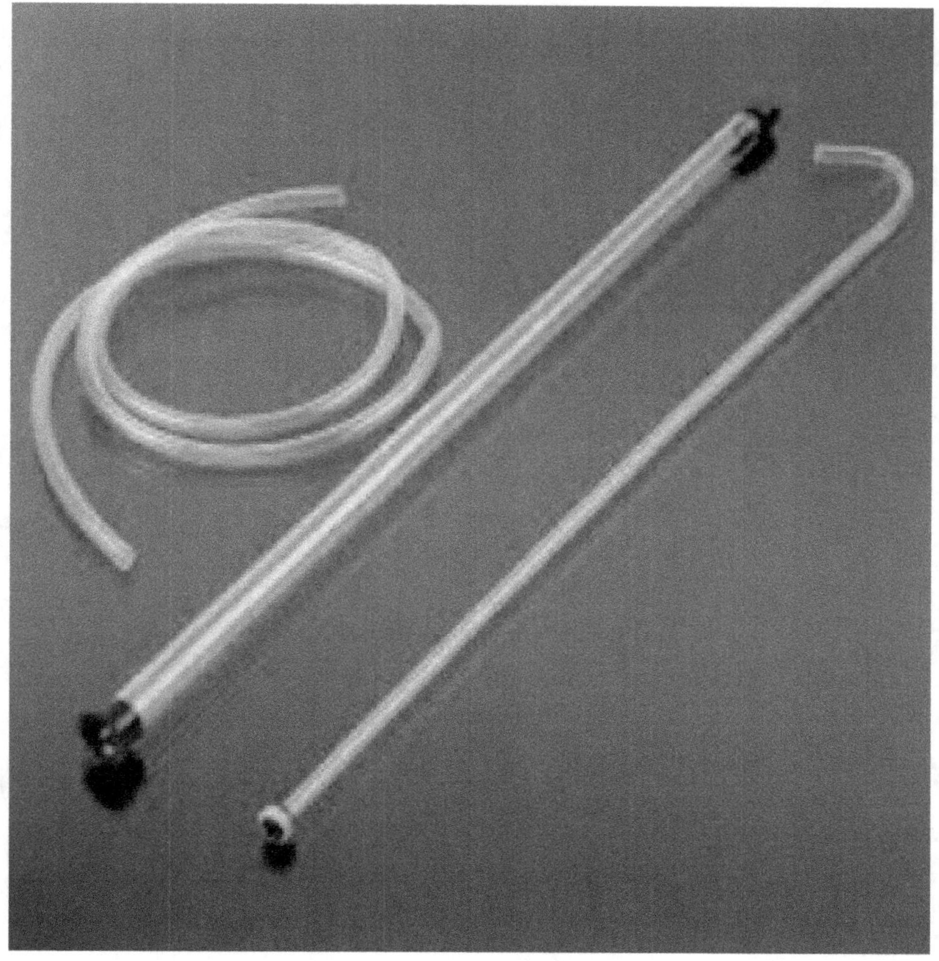

Siphon Pump Pictured above..

The Siphon pump is Simple to use once you get the hang of things.

First insert the Vinyl tubing onto the bent end of the clear tubing, then carefully insert the other end into the open portion of the Collection tube. Taking the Cap off of the discharge end of the Collection tube, hold the discharge over the opening of the Clean Carboy, Compress the rod inside the collection chamber, then in-

serting the vinyl tubing into the fermented wine pull up on the bent arm, you should see fluid move through tubing and into the clean carboy you may need to pump a couple of times transfer down to the sediment, you can expect leaving a bit of wine behind to not pick up sediment this is normal.

*5) HYDROMETER AND ITS USE IN WINE-MAKING

Perhaps the most important tool in Wine-making, the hydrometer is Used to not only Measure Specific Gravity but to Follow the Fermentation Progress of the wine. In following chapters I will discuss how to use it in depth later in this book

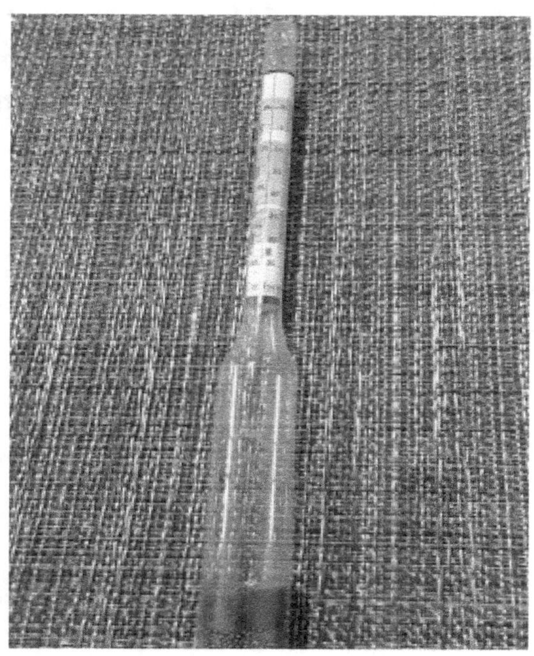

Hydrometer used in reading Specific   Gravity in Wine-making

*6) COLLECTION JAR DESIGNED FOR HYDROMETER

 The Collection jar is also an important part of every Winemakers arsenal. The jar is filled ¾ full to take specific gravity reading (SG) of the wine or beer to chart progress of the fermentation and also to determine alcohol Content. If you are Taking an (SG) reading of your wine, I highly recommend that after taking the reading to either pour the sample out, or if preferred take a tasting of your wine but never add back to the must to avoid risk of contamination of the whole batch. Spring Water is used to Top off the Wine prior to bottling ..

Glass Collection Jar for hydrometer

Pictured above,

*7) PLASTIC MEASURING SPOONS –

available virtually everywhere, plastic measuring Spoons are Necessary to add ingredients throughout the wine-making Process.

*8) PLASTIC FUNNELS -

Another important element, Plastic Funnels should be Kept on hand for various steps in the Wine-making Process. I personally use them when Bottling the Wine to avoid Spills, also used in back sweetening wine with sugar while in the Carboy.

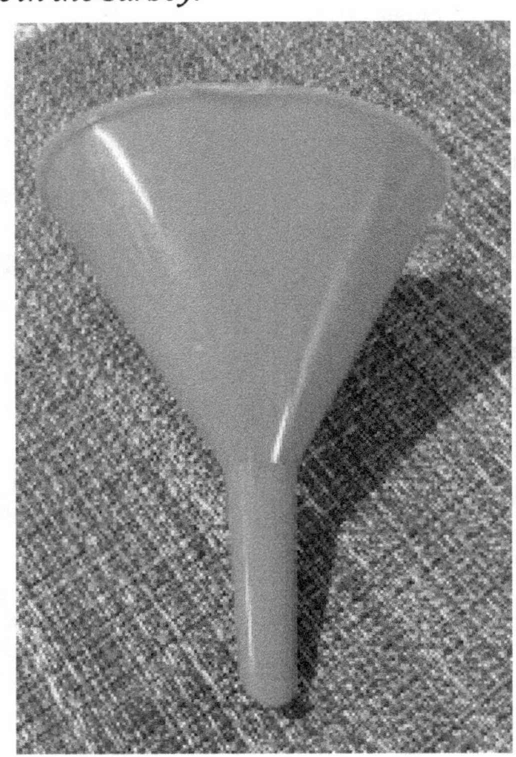

*9) YEAST-

The Most MVP of the Wine making toolkit is yeast. There are many Different types of yeast for home brewing but perhaps the Most common are regular bread yeast in the red, white and blue packages pictured, or Champaign yest shown in the Yellow Satchels

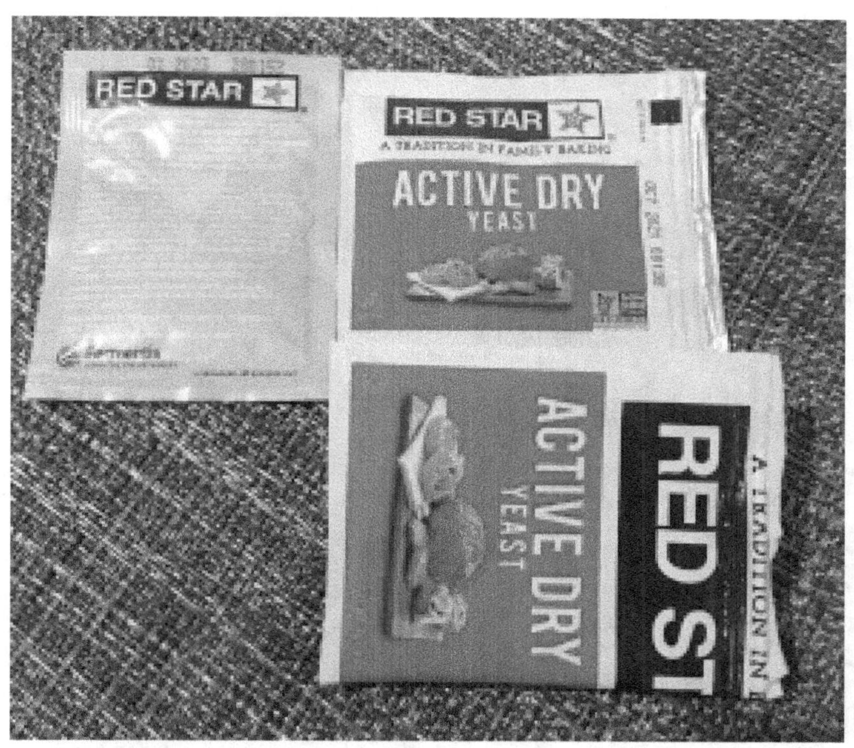

When using bread yeast its important to understand that bread yeast will typically give a wine with a lower Alcohol Content

*(3-7% Max), and cannot tolerate large amounts of sugar in the must, large amounts of Sugar will Overwhelm the yeast Causing it to die off early leaving behind a Wine with low alcohol Content and too sweet. Champaign yeast is better at heavier concentrations of Sugar and will produce high Alcohol content Wines in upward of 14-15% ABV Wines (**ABV = Alcohol by Volume**)... If I'm experimenting with a new recipe, I Save my good yeast, lower the amt. Of Sugar added and pitch bread yeast*

*10) WINE CORKER-

Self Explanatory the Wine Corker is A very Important tool needed in finishing off your Run of Wine. It can typically be intimidating at first and as you look at it the "Claws" are designed to grip the bottle under the flange and the cork is loaded through the side after tool is in Place. I highly recommend Practicing on an empty bottle prior to bottling your first batch, it can be cumbersome to use and we don't want to spill any valuable homemade wine we have been waiting on.

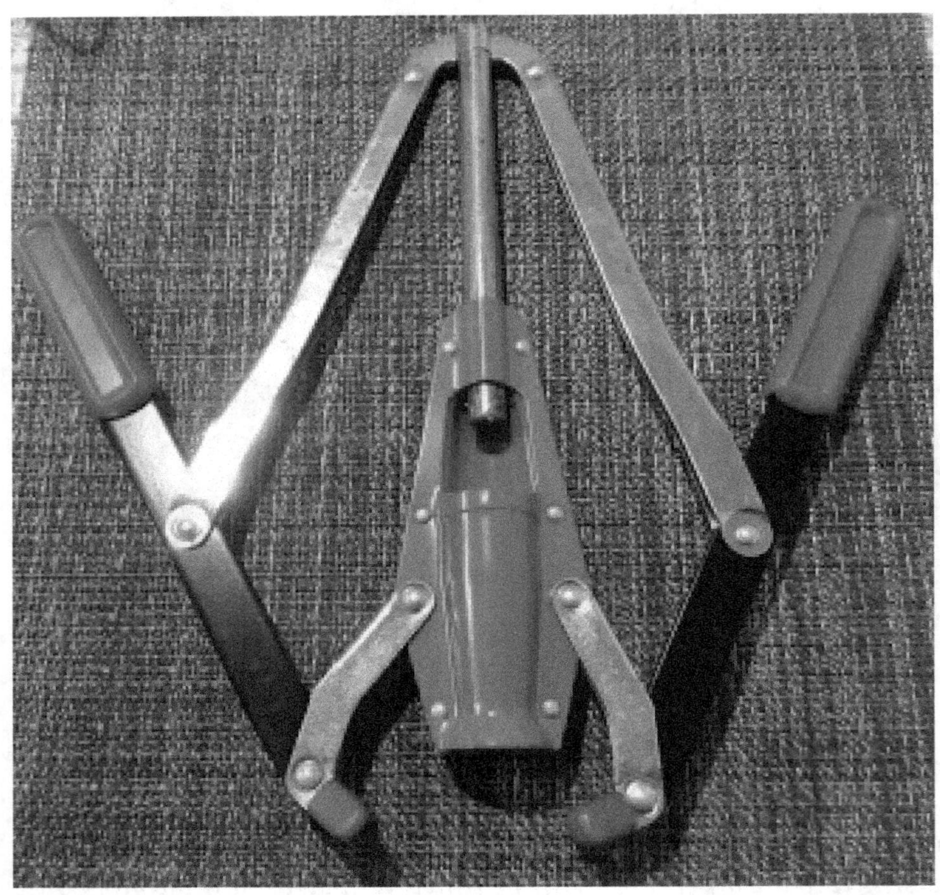

*After Cork is Loaded through the Opening on the Side carefully applying pressure to both handles pushing downward slowly you will cork your bottle. To this day I prefer to bottle either on my workbench or in the sink. I recommend the sink at first as its easy to splash until you learn the balance of this tool. It's not at all hard and does not require much pressure **(You Can Do It!)***

*11) WINE CORKS-

*ine Corks are Essential to Seal off your Creation and Save for a later date. While you can drink Right away, the Wine Won't develop full Flavor for 3-6 Months. **I personally Use #7 Corks, 1-1/2" Long.** After Corking your Bottles it's Important to leave the Wine Bottles in the upright Position for the first 5-7 days then after they settle, to store them on the side to help keep the corks wet and not letting them dry out. Store your Wine in a Conditioned Space no Warmer Then Mid 60's and ideally in an electric Wine Cooler.

*12) YEAST NUTRIENTS-

When the little beastie's (Yeast Work away at Converting Sugar into alcohol they get tired, grow weary and sometimes die off before all of the Sugar has been converted into alcohol. **Yeast Nutrient is important to fortify the yeast giving it the nutrients to Complete the process.** *A good rule of thumb is as Follows,* **a must pitched with bread yeast should contain no more than 1 pound of Sugar if not wanting to add yeast Nutrients** *because* **bread yeast will only convert 1.25LBS of Sugar without being overwhelmed** *and leaving you with a Wine which is too Sweet!*

If using Champaign Yeast, Champaign Yeast will Convert Most of a 2 LB Concentration of Sugar into alcohol. If a Higher

Concentration (14% VS. 12% ABV Alcohol), I Highly recommend the yeast Nutrient to *ensure a good Fermentation.*

Above is a typical 1 OZ Jar of yeast Nutrient

FINISHING SULPHITES 101-

After A month or Better of Hard Work, Racking your Wines (Transferring from carboy to Carboy) and Preparing to Bottle the Final Step it for Storage and prevent Spoilage. Prior to Bottling the Wine in your Pretty Bottles and Corking it we need to add two ingredients lets have a Look below.

Potassium metabisulfite -is added once you ensure all bubbling in the airlock has stopped and Wine is ready to be Racked One last time to remove all Yeast Nutrients. After The Final Rack I would highly Recommend letting the Wine rest and off-gas before adding your final ingredients. The thought behind this is to avoid the bottle popping its cork once bottled because of pressure. Also recommended to let it rest once ingredients are mixed into the Wine. The Rest Period Should be One week after each process.

Potassium metabisulfite is stirred in to kill off all remaining yeast fermentation that cannot be seen. You can expect a tiny amount of sediment to fall from the wine after added also clearing the wine. Again Rack the Wine.

If you taste your wine and decide after clearing Sediment that it's too bitter and requires some back Sweetening to make it more acceptable to Consume you must First add by stirring in Potassium Sorbet That prevents Fermentation to Kick off due to Sugar being added.

Lets take a Look at our Finishing Ingredients Below, Please Follow directions on bottle labels to get the correct amount of each.

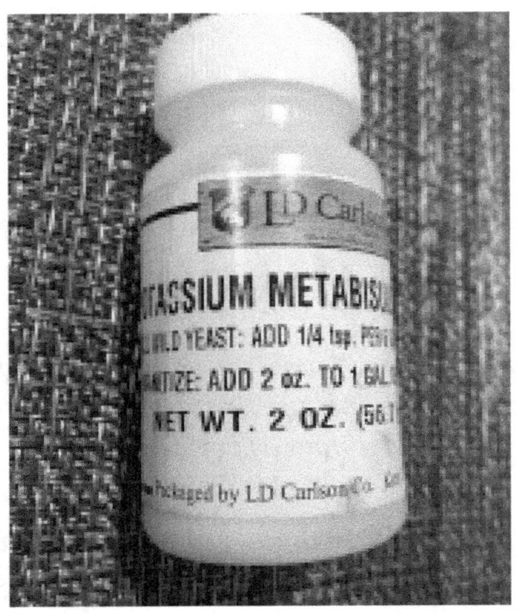

Potassium metabisulfite above

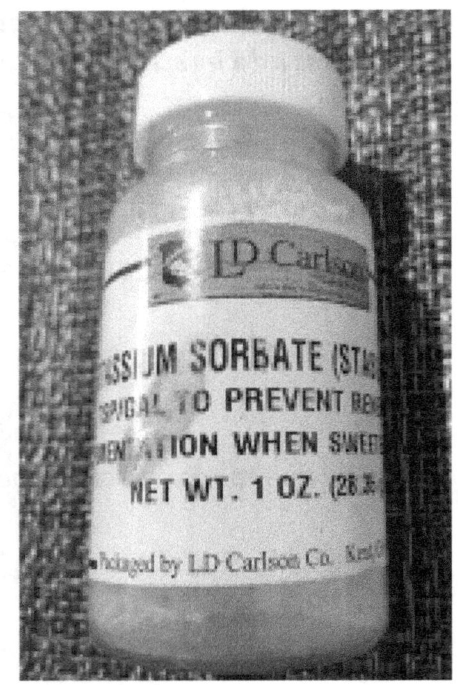

* ***Potassium Sorbate***

*WINE BOTTLES-

One of The Final things Needed into your Supply Closet is Clean, Fresh Wine bottles. It Doesn't matter if new or Used but Sanitation is the key here. If you decide to use a used bottle, be sure to sanitize the inside with sanitizer. Also you will probably want to remove any labels if using a Used bottle.

Care should be taken in Removing the label, the best way I have found to remove the label is to completely fill the wine bottle with water for weight, insert the cork or any cork as far into the bottle by hand as possible to keep Soap out! Soap remnant will ruin the flavor of your Wines. Next plug the Sink and fill with warm water adding just 4-5 drops of dish soap to break adhesive on the bottle. Soak for about 20 minutes and Label should easily peel off. Rinse bottle and pour water out that's inside. You are all set.

750 ML Wine Bottles

Wine Bottles Continued-

750 Ml Wine Bottles are Sold at Most Brewery Supply Stores each or by the Case. Typically Bottles are Sold for Under $2.00 each or under $20.00 per case. Friends saving Bottles are even better yet with minor prep work used bottles work fine.

Another note and a nice touch,

from time to time its not uncommon to bring a bottle of wine to a dinner party or potentially a six pack of beer. Another option for your fantastic homemade wines is to purchase a clear wine bottle with a flip top lid to bring your beverage for others to enjoy.

In these bottles wine should be refrigerated and I would not plan on a long term storage, a max of about 7 days. Its easy to rinse out and bring home with you after the dinner party.

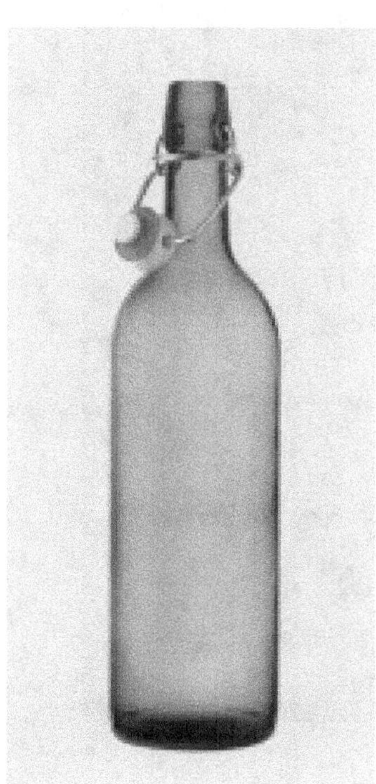

*CAMPDEN TABLETS-

The Final Ingredient-

The Last ingredient to add to your wonderful Wine is **Campden Tablets.** *Campden tablets are added to Wine to Sanitize the wine killing any bacteria that may be in the Wine. Crush one Tablet by putting it into a tablespoon, taking another tablespoon and push down on top of the tablet applying pressure to the top spoon. After crushed stir into the Wine Until fully dissolved.*

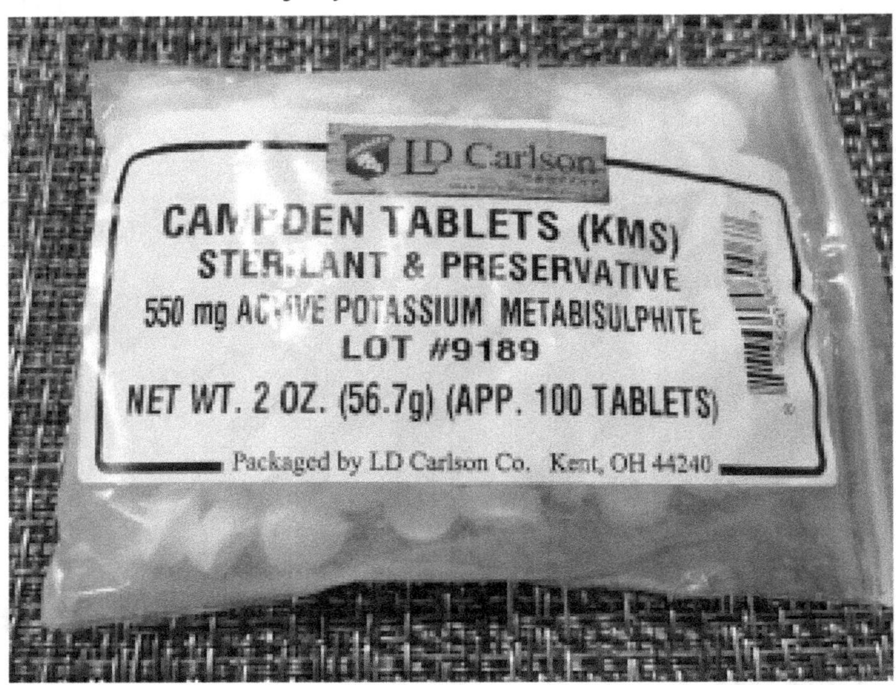

Campden Tablets. Add one tablet per batch

CHAPTER IV –

Getting Started*, Now You Have all of your tools gathered, it's time to Start Planning your First Batch of Wine. So the Big Decision and fun one is, what flavor is your first batch going to be, there are options of either making Wine from Fruit juice found in the Isles of Grocery Stores Nation Wide, Or to peel fruit and make homemade wine from fruit bought at local grocery stores, but because you are just getting Started We are going to outline in this book, Making wine from fruit-juice with great Success in doing so.*

Choosing the Juice-

When you are at the store, Choosing a fruit Juice there are a few important things to keep in mind/ know.. first of all the Size to Target is 64oz. 64 oz, equates to roughly one half Gallon so in order to make one Gallon of Wine buy Two jugs of Juice. The Plastic jugs are also very helpful in racking your wines. When you go down the juice Isle there are things that qualify the juice as a good candidate for wine and also not so great for your wine-making, at this time please take a piece of paper and jot down items I have highlighted in red so as you browse through juices you will have a "Cheat Sheet" to help in the Selection Process.

So First, *(No Diet Juices,)*No Natural Sugar means no Alcohol Production! Next there *(cannot be any Vegetable juices added)* and also read the label to make sure it Says *(No preservatives added Preservatives will kill yeast and juice will not ferment correctly).* Next try to Find Juices that Say Made from 100% Real Fruit Juice, I have made wine with juices containing as little as 10% Fruit juice but better quality is to be had if you get as close to 100% Pure Juice. Another important factor in Wine-making is that Citrus Wine can be made with more Complex additives, but I recommend *(Avoiding Citrus Juice)* while Learning the Process.

Choosing the Juice Continued-

Perhaps the final and most important Factor is grams of Sugar per serving which is very important to know, when making your must. I will not buy unsweetened wine because this adds to the amount of Sugar required for the Conversion into Wine and its simply not worth the headache. Choose a fruit juice that has between 10 grams of sugar per serving up to 20. ***I prefer more sugar per serving on the label of the juice and have developed a threshold when it comes to adding Sugar see below:***

Sugar Content In Juice for Wine-making-

(5-10 grams of sugar per serving)- if the label on the juice indicates this amount of sugar per serving then an extra one half pound is added in step increments to not overwhelm yeast. *Step increments meaning starting the must with the standard 1-1/2 LB of sugar added then slowly over the period of seven days fold the additional 1/2 LB of sugar into the must. Extreme Care and Caution should be taken not to pour sugar all at once instead pour and stir slowly as the sugar will have a foaming effect on the yeast. If you are making 1-2 gallons of wine with unsweetened juice I recommend your fermenter is a 5 gallon food grade bucket with lid to avoid spill overs.*

10-15 grams of sugar per serving– my standard amount of 1-1/2 Lbs of Sugar is added to the Juice.

16-20 grams of Sugar per Serving (Ideal)- Only 1-1/2 LBS of Sugar added to the fruit-juice for my Wine-making

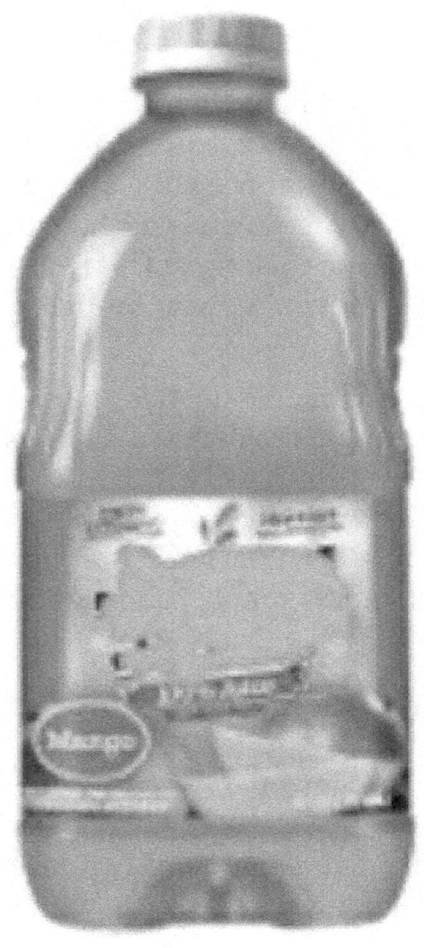

Above, what a 64 ounce Container of Juice looks

__like__ for Reference. Always save these Containers, you Should have four on hand to help with Racking the wines.

Next on the shopping list is Granulated Sugar,

There are so Many options when it comes to Sugar these days but the Container Sizes do matter when it Comes to wine-making. So for all proper practices I am focusing on two separate sizes for our wine-making, 2 Lb and Four Pound Bags.

I personally Prefer 2 LB bags and keep six, two pound bags on hand at all times. When bringing home before storing them take all six, and with a **Sharpe Marker, draw a line across the middle of the sugar bags for reference of how much to add when mixing Must.** Two of the Six should have Four reference marks one being in the middle and the other two marks spitting the distance between the middle of the bag and the ends. This mark represents ¼ of a pound of sugar, do this to two of the bags and **mark on them (Back-sweetening only).**

About Folding Sugar into your fruit juice -

by now I'm almost positive all of my readers are puzzled about all this sugar being added to already sweet fruit juice, ut please Keep in mind the yeast is going after this mixture Converting sugar into alcohol and C02 as it works away, so the end result is going to be a wine that has a surprisingly smooth taste and packs a bit of a punch. If your first batch turns out too sweet, don't despair, it can happen to all beginners and it has happened to me as well. No need to throw it out, set it to the side, it can be reused in another batch purposely mixed with low sugar to absorb sweetness.

Sugar Recap the followup.

To Recap on all of this, my standard one gallon of Wine is Given 1-1/2 Pounds of Sugar. A rookie mistake when making wine for the first time is to cruise the internet and when reading that a recipe calls for 2 cups of Sugar that Someone actually uses a Measuring Cup to pour Sugar in I have always added sugar to my fruit juice via, the weight of the bag meaning no measuring cup period.

For Reference only one pound of Sugar is Equal to approximately 2-1/4 Cups of Sugar. I always Try to leave a bit of sugar in the bottom of the bag to avoid making a must packed with too much sugar for the yeast to work with.

Sugar Consideration with yeast-

Another helpful hint I would like to pass along is that if buying Juice on Sale Somewhere for $0.99 I will always pitch my bread yeas into the must and go light on the sugar addition to the juice so my cheap yeast will fully process my cheap juice creating a 4-7% wine. Always save your more expensive Champaign yeast (available online) for Juices with higher quality. Finally Grape juice makes good strong wines, however I caution that if going with grape juice I would error on the light side of sugar and as you take your readings during fermentation you can sneak a sip to see if its too bland and fold small amounts of more sugar in to avoid creating a red wine that's too sweet to drink.

CHAPTER V

Congratulations on this very special day. Today we are going to get your very first run of wine started and about 45 days from now, give or take you will be putting this vintage in your wine rack to enjoy on a very special day or give as a birthday gift. Lets get started.

Wine Making is kind of like photography in one sense, that it cannot be rushed and I cant recommend enough to choose a day where you wont be bothered or sidetracked so you can both prepare and learn at the same time. I recommend to choose a clean area near water either in a kitchen next to the sink or possibly the laundry area if your laundry room has a sink. Additionally a clean work surface is a necessity to lay out your needed tools and ingredients. I personally prefer a small fiberglass folding table as its just about the right height for what you are about to do.

Next take a small plastic container and reading the directions on your sanitizer solution bottle, mix up approx I gallon of cleaner and set aside as you will also be cleaning throughout this entire process. Next get your food grade fermenter open the lid and pour just enough sanitizer in to cover the bottom about one inch and with a clean cloth, give the inside a good cleaning. Rinse vigorously with warm water and dry.

Next, open up all of your fruit juice Containers and pour into the fermenter. Care should be taken when pouring juices to gently tilt bottle to the side over the bucket but not completely upside down. The reason being, is that pulp or sediment may have settled to the bottom of the container which we want to avoid introducing into our must. (**This is also known as racking when transferring wine from one carboy to the next without a siphon pump**). It's OK and to be expected to have a bit of juice remaining in the bottom of both fruit juice containers, after all juice is poured, rinse out the jugs and then sanitize them by pouring a bit of your sanitizer in each, put lid on and vigorously shake them. Then remove lids, rinse with warm water and lay upside down without lids on towel to dry.

Making your first batch Continued-

The Next Step in preparing our Must is to locate a Plastic spoon long enough to Stir as we fold in Sugar. Metal Spoons, I would not Recommend because metal can Give off an off taste into the Juice, and Avoid Wooden spoons as a wood spoon is not completely sealed and could contain by product of cooking and smells that transfer into the wine. Keep mixing until the juice dissolves all of the sugar. Once completely blended cover and set aside.

Depending on the fruit Juice you are using Slowly fold in the Sugar by Stirring as you add ¼ pound at a Time. (***Do not heat on a stove, this will cause off tastes as the juice warms)..***

Before adding the yeast starter to your Must-

Records are very important when Making Wine so you Can determine your Alcohol Content of the Final Product. SO before getting Started you Need to get the hydrometer out for your first reading also known as the Specific Gravity Reading. This Reading is obtained by pouring must into the Collection jar to aprox 3/4 full then carefully inserting the hydrometer down into solution with the number graduation scale facing you (See Below For Example).. Take the reading and jot down.. **please note when taking the reading it will be below the 1.000 line so if you are showing 80 on the scale the specific gravity reading will be 1.080**

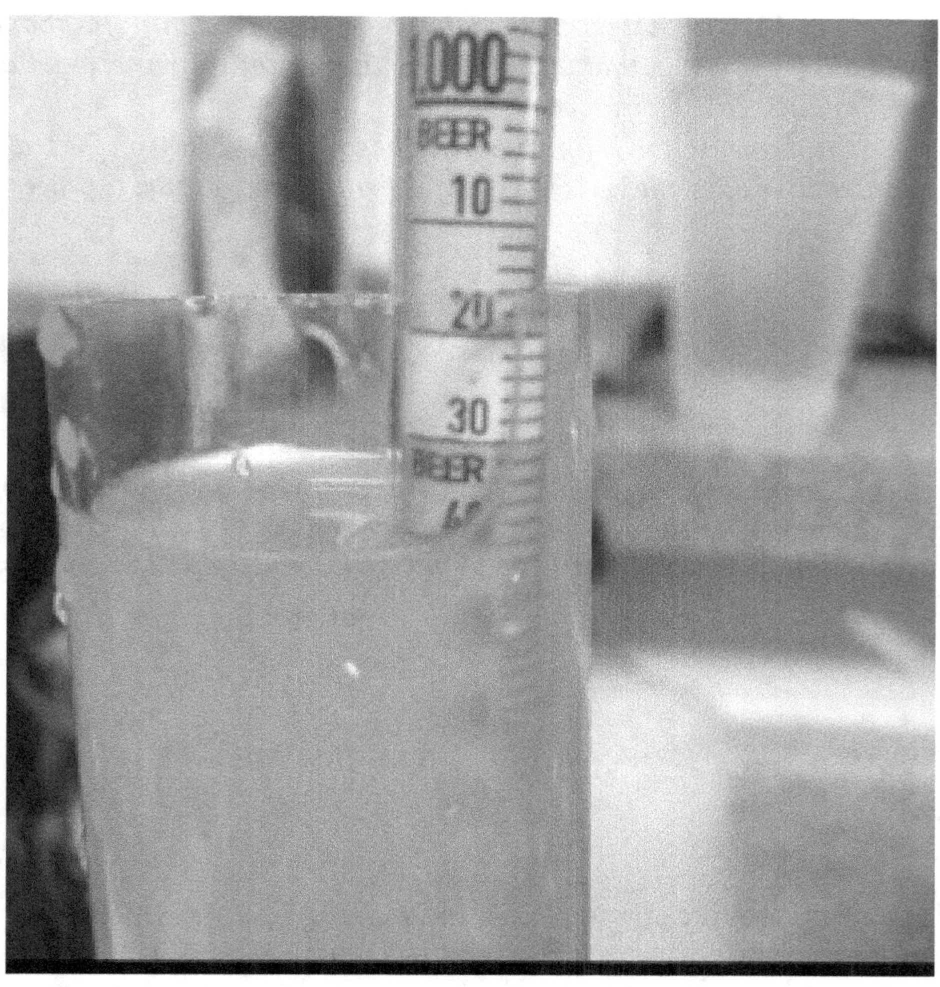

above, always shake the collection jar for accurate readings. Never leave hydrometer smashed against side of jar it will cause a false reading. This reading is 1.060

Hydrometers tell us four crucial things, but only if we pay attention and write down what the readings are every time we take them.

First, *your hydrometer reading on day one lets you know your wine has the right amount of sugar to ferment out and give you an alcohol content appropriate to style. If the reading is too low or too high, double-check that the wine is at the right level (6-US gallons/22.7 litres). If it is, then give the wine a brutal stirring. Sugar can settle out on the bottom and throw a reading off.*

Second, readings taken during fermentation will show that fermentation is proceeding. Watching for foam or bubbles in the airlock doesn't tell you anything except that CO2 gas is coming out of the wine, and the gravity may not be changing while that happens. Your hydrometer never lies!
Next, your hydrometer will tell you when the fermentation is finished. After it gets below 1.000 on the scale and then stays at that point for three consecutive days, the kit is finished fermenting and it's safe to proceed to the next step.

Figuring out your alcohol level

Finally your hydrometer will let you calculate how much alcohol your wine contains. If you wrote down the SG number at the beginning, and compare it to the number at the end, you'll see how much sugar was used up. To figure out how much alcohol that made, *all you have to do is multiply the change in gravity by 131. Here's how:*

Finishing Gravity	0.998
Starting Gravity	1.088
Difference	0.900
0.900 x 131	11.79% ABV

Taking care of your hydrometer

Hydrometers need to be cleaned and sanitized like all pieces of wine-making equipment. Hydrometers need to be treated gently: all of them used to be made from glass, just like thermometers. This meant that a minor bump or drop and they broke instantly. Nowadays, however, we've got an alternative, the *Herculometer*. Made of Poly-carbonate plastic, it's much tougher than glass – it's not indestructible, but it can take a few bumps and knocks and still be there when you need it.

To Prepare the Yeast for fermentation, get either a Large glass cup or a mason jar ready. With a small saucepan full of water put on the stove to heat. Carefully watching with a thermometer heat water until it reaches 90 degree's Fahrenheit. Once water reaches temp, stir in 2 tablespoons of Sugar until dissolved then open your yeast and pour one packet into the water, stir gently and let sit for 45 minutes to hydrate. When rechecking the yeast, it should of developed a foamy cake on top about one inch thick. Taking the jar introduce this into the fruit juice by lightly stirring in. next step sanitize the jar you pitched the yeast in. after I add yeast to a must I give it overnight to multiply in the bucket by covering the bucket out of the way, with a towel and not the lid for 8 hours. Covering too soon does not give yeast the oxygen needed to multiply. When you remove the towel aprox 6-8 hours later you should see vigorous activity bubbling and light foam on the Surface. You are now fermenting that first batch of Wine!

After the 6-8 hour window carefully Snap the bucket's lid on and take the airlock and fill with water only ensuring that water is even on both sides you might have to turn back and fourth as you fill the airlock. Once water is up to the line on both side plug the airlock into the bung installed in the lid. This will keep debris and pests out of your wine. It should start bubbling very rapidly and do so for about the first 3-7 days.

After the excitement of Starting your first batch subsides, I highly recommend getting in the habit of every three days or so checking on the fermentation, first fermentation will go anywhere from 3 days to 2 weeks evident by activity in the airlock. When the bubble release in the airlock slows to one bubble every 30 seconds or so, first fermentation has completed and its time to rack to a Carboy. The Term Racking Simply means carefully transferring to a new container being careful not to transfer sediment with it. Racking can be done one of two ways, first a plastic funnel in the mouth of the new carboy **(Funnel being sanitized first!)** with the Lid off of your fermentation bucket, slowly and without stopping pour a slow stream inside the funnel watching with caution to not let yeast sediments through (Reason for slow steady motion)...

Before you Rack to a Carboy and depending on the quantity of wine you have started make sure the carboy has the capacity to hold the wine, if not two smaller carboy's are OK but set them both up side by side, a funnel already in the mouth of each carboy, the reason for this is if you are using the pour method vs. siphon pump, you never want to set wine down while preparing second carboy. Doing so will stir up sediment that will pour right into your fresh carboy, you don't want that!

CHAPTER VI

After Racking reinsert your Airlock and Mark the calendar on the day of your Racking. Second Fermentation goes for around two weeks. You will be able to tell by the airlock when when it looks like fermentation has wrapped up. Never assume on this! Once Bubbling has Stopped you will want to take an *(SG or Specific Gravity Reading)* to see where on the scale the fermentation is at. If you are at 0.998 then fermentation has Completed or if real close you are ready to bottle. Allow the Wine to sit for a few days to see if it clears.

If not you will have to add a Clearing or Fining agent and its Completely Safe to Consume in the wines. Be sure to read package for directions and adjust according to your batch. An example of a fining agent can be seen here not every batch of wine turns out perfectly in fact problems can arrise and I will discuss Stuck fermetation in the Next Chapter including how to troubleshoot and fix this annoyance. Problems with Fermentation are Usually Caused by one of three factors.

1) Temperature in the surrounding area-

Too warm and yeast dies off, too cool and it will Suspend

2) Too Much Sugar with the wrong yeast, *bread yeast will not ferment a large amount of Sugars I recommend not Over a Pound*

3) Failure to add Yeast Nutrient to the Must

CHAPTER VII-

If you have racked your wine into a carboy and looking at the surface after a couple of days, it looks as though everything has come to a screeching halt, also known as stuck fermentation we need to find out why.

First we need to gather a couple of things. Here we are going to need the following items-

Collection Jar

Hydrometer

your notebook and pen

a flashlight

so the first step is to check the surrounding room temp. if its below 68 degree Fahrenheit there is a good chance the fermentation has suspended because yeast thrive in temps between 68-74 degrees Fahrenheit. To Avoid making other members of your household miserable with a temp variance for the wine, find a new location with a steady temp. to jump start the process after moving the carboy lay a heating pad under the carboy and put on the lowest temp setting for about 30 mins. Come back and observe, did that work? Observe the surface of the wine inside the carboy for activity.

While you cant rely on a visual to indicate fermentation a sure fire method to visually check is to shine the flashlight into the carboy and look closely above the light for tiny bubbles escaping to the surface this indicates fermentation!

If the process above did not work ensure your carboy is not setting on the bare concrete, this will cool the wine too much. I put a box beneath wine first or a small block of wood. Step number two and perhaps the most important step, draw a collection jar of wine and take a (SG) reading, or specific gravity reading. This indicates if the must has finished fermentation. A reading close to 0.998 will indicate this. If its no where near this number then the fermentation is indeed stuck and more drastic measures are needed to kick it off again, please read on..

Because anything above 0.998 indicates Sugar in the Wine we are going to attempt to stir in ¼ cup of yeast nutrient along with ½ a packet of yeast (Fresh) to attempt to kick things off again.

Let the wine rest a day or so then return to the wine with your flashlight, do you see bubbles? If so then congrats the problem has been solved if not the third and final aggressive action. Because too much sugar may have overwhelmed your yeast too early if on the second day of throwing more yeast has not worked we are going to divide the quantity of wine made in two or in two separate carboys.

After the wine has been separated we are going to add 1 full cup of spring-water (not distilled water) to each carboy and take another (SG) test, look to see if that has bought the number closer to 0.998 (we never want to dilute too much) but the idea is too make sugars less for the new yeast.

Give this a week to ferment then take a look again. If you notice a partial clearing starting from top to bottom your wine is finishing up. If after this time nothing has happened with the fermentation, dont throw the wine out! It might be a bit sweet but you can make a secondary batch purposely with 2/3 less sugar and blend with this sweet wine to still have a decent wine.

CHAPTER VIII-

Finishing Touches wrapping up-

the part you have been waiting for its time to sample to see what the flavor of your final product is going to be. You have some options and if your wine has turned out too sweet please do not despair. If its got a semi sweet body then it's best served as a desrt wine and chilled. If its just plain too sweet below are some solutions to adjust taste. The trick in adjusting taste is that we never want to dilute wine too much with water and ruin it. A tried and true trick to the home wine enthusiast making fruit juice wine, is that if its too sweet. It can be diluted with a dry white wine to take sweetness away.

The Other option in front of us is to make another batch using the same juice but cut the sugar content way back and mix our sweet wine in with it, this preserves the flavor you were originally shooting for without adding white wines. ***This is the method I prefer..***

The Other Option is too use pure spring water from the Grocery store to dillute slightly. I will caution you to do so in small amounts and not to be too heavy handed with the water jug, there's no solution for dilution!

A final word on flavoring your final product-

There is no right or wrong way in crafting your own wine, never let anyone influence you in your pursuit of wine-making! The only enemy in wine-making is bacteria, and using best cleanliness practices with your equipment will produce great tasting wines!

If your wine is too bitter in taste-

Occasionally you will make a batch that's dry with very little sweetness. There is a solution here as well.

If you decide sugar is needed I caution you here, that while rare, adding sugar can kick off a fermentation again, so with this being said we are going to add products to not only kill yeast, but to prevent fermentation from kicking off by back-sweetening, here's how that works, after you rack your wines and they are waiting in a carboy, you are going to first add your Potassium Metabisululfite which when stirred in, will kill all wild yeast in the carboy. Give this a day to rest. Next prior to sweetening add in the potassium sorbate, which prevents re-fermentation from kicking off. Let this rest another day.

next its time to add sugar. **Caution to not add too much sugar is needed here so I recommend only adding the Sugar at 1 Tablespoon at a time. Mix in thoroughly and taste. Sweeten as needed**

IX- Bottling your Wine

Now we are ready to bottle your wine. For this you are going to need the appropriate number of wine bottles be sure to rinse them well. Also needed you will need your Corker and Corks, and Finally this Fermenter and Spigot. Lets Finish up!

To start, Sanitize your fermenting bucket well with your sanitizing solution also sanitize bottles and rinse out with clean water. After all cleaned up taking your Carboys one at a time add to the fermenting bucket then sanitize the carboys well. I never fill fermenter to the top only ¾ full. Position the fermenter on an object over the Sink with spigot over the sink itself. Next one at a time fill your wine bottles (Exciting Part!)

Wine bottles should never be filled to the top as the cork is going to be pushed down inside and will take up space. For proper amount in bottle I recommend holding the cork on the outside to see how far down it goes in with a piece of tape mark bottle where the bottom of the cork ends. When you fill the bottle you want ideally ¾" between the Cork and the top of the wine for aging. Nice job on your wine run, what flavor is next on the agenda?

CONCLUSION-

Wine making is a very rewarding hobby . My Goal someday is to build a beautiful wine-rack /Cellar in my basement featuring only my own Vintages.

I will Caution that while it' s very rewarding to do, there are those who will automatically Judge you thinking there is a drinking problem or you are an "alcoholic"…just ignore the negativity, for this reason I don't talk much about it outside my circle of Friends.

Crafting your Own alcohol is fun, creating your own recipes and sharing a bottle at the next Dinner party you go to-why not Bring a Bottle. Watch for my Future books as I am planning to write a book on Using real fruits to make wines (a longer process) I hope to write very soon.

Also I plan to Share Recipes in the very near future with what has turned out to be fantastic in wines. Be sure to check back

www.ingramcontent.com/pod-product-compliance
Lightning Source LLC
Chambersburg PA
CBHW081826250726
48657CB00011B/3500